WHAT HAPPENED NEXT?

GREAT

DISASTERS

Valerie Nott

FRANKLIN WATTS

NEW YORK • CHICAGO • LONDON • TORONTO • SYDNEY

© 1995 Franklin Watts

Franklin Watts
95 Madison Avenue
New York, NY 10016

Library of Congress Cataloging-in -Publication Data

Nott, Valerie
    Great disasters / Valerie Nott.
        p. cm. - (What happened next?)
    Includes index.
    ISBN 0-531 - 14360-0
    1. Disasters - Juvenile literature. I. Title. II Series.
    D24. N68 1995
    904'.7 - dc20   94-39207
                            CIP AC

10 9 8 7 6 5 4 3 2 1

Series editor: Belinda Weber
Designer: Cassedy Design Company; Edward Kinsey; Nina Kingsbury
Illustrators: David Penfound; Ed Dovey
Picture researchers: Diana Morris, Matthew Parselle

Photographs: Bridgeman Art Library: 11t (Private Collection), 12t (British Museum), 13tl Villa dei Misteri Pompeii,
15b Museo e Gallerie Nazionale di Capodimonte, 17t British Library, 18c Bibliotheque Nationale, 18-19b Trinity
College Cambridge, 21t Musee Minicipal Berger; John Burbidge/Science Photo Library: 22tr; Dr Jeremy
Burgess/Science Photo Library: 5c; Bruce Coleman Ltd © Andy Purcell 21b, © Hans Reinhard 15t, 37c;
CNRI/Science Photo Library: 22t; Martin Dorhn/Science Photo Library: 19c; e t archive: 11c, 13tr Naples Museum,
14 t Capitoline Museum, Rome, 17c University of Prague, 33t; Mary Evans Picture Library: 16t, 22c, 23bl, 23bc, 25tl,
25tr, 26b, 28t, 28cl, 29t, 36c, 40t, 40bl; Simon Fraser/Science Photo Library: 10bl; Biraudon/Bridgeman Art Library:
17b Musée Condé Chantilly; Francois Gohier/Science Photo Library: 10c; Robert Harding Picture Library: 28b;
Harland & Wolff Collection, Ulster Folk & Transport Museum: 27t; Sonia Halliday Photographs: 11b; Hulton Deutsch:
4b, 19t, 20t, 23t, 23c, 23br, 24bl, 29bl, 29br, 30t, 30bl, 30 br, 31t, 32b, 34t, 34cl, 34c, 36-7b, 38t, 39b, 40c; Illustrated
London News Picture Library: 24t; Lauros-Giraudon/Bridgeman Art Library: 20b Musée Condé Chantilly;
NASA/Science Photo Library: 8t, 10t; John Reader/Science Photo Library: 5t; Rex Features/Sipa Press: 28cr; Royal
Aeronautical Society: 32t; Spectrum Colour Library: 38b; Geoff Tomkinson/Science Photo Library: 22b; Zefa: Cover,
4t, 8b, 9t, 9b, 10br, 16c, 16bl, 16br, 26t, 33b, 35t, 39t, 40br.

Printed in Belgium.

CONTENTS

The dictionary defines disaster as a sudden great misfortune, a calamity or ill luck, or an event of a distressing or ruinous nature. The word disaster conjures up an image of something awful.

Disasters can occur on a personal level. Coping with and living with such disasters is part of everyday life. Some disasters, however, happen on a much larger scale, and for those involved who survive, it changes their lives forever.

Some icebergs look beautiful – like scuptures floating on the sea. Could something this beautiful be deadly?

WHAT IS A DISASTER?

CHANGING PEOPLE'S LIVES

Throughout history, some of the disasters that have happened have directly affected the lives of thousands of people. Even in Biblical times,

During prehistoric times, pterosaurs ruled the skies. Why are there none around today?

disasters such as floods, famines, and even plagues of locusts occurred which completely changed peoples lives, leaving them to cope with both changed lifestyles and environments.

WATCHING THE NEWS

Today, we are all too well aware of each new disaster as it's brought to our attention by the news media. Wherever such

disasters occur we see the heartbreak and pain, and although we may not be involved, we feel the emotions of the people who are.

TRAGIC SYMBOLS

Disasters are all around us and always have been. Most take the world by surprise and can neither be predicted nor anticipated. The very fact that they are unexpected makes them

particularly tragic. The great loss of life and the shock they produce remain far beyond living memory. They become tragic symbols of human vulnerability.

WHY DO WE REMEMBER?

What makes one particular disaster live on in memory and myth? Great loss of life? This might vary from a few dozen lives to thousands lost. Totally unexpected shock? Some disasters are "expected" but are still shocking when they suddenly strike. Human vulnerability and a feeling of helplessness may make disasters memorable,

During the black death, doctors in Europe wore special clothes to protect themselves. But did these clothes help?

or maybe it's the triumph of survivors against great odds that makes them stay in our minds. By looking at some of the great disasters of history and asking what made these disasters important, we might discover why their images remain so clear.

TERRIBLE LIZARDS

Masses of blue-green algae clump together to form stromalolites. These are among the oldest organic remains ever found, dating from 2,000 to 3,000 million years ago.

The planet Earth is the ideal place for life to develop. It is just at the right distance from the sun, and is well supplied with life-giving water and oxygen.

About five billion years ago, the Earth took shape out of a vast, hot, spinning cloud of gas. Over millions of years, Earth cooled, becoming first liquid and then solid. Torrential rains lashed the cooling rocks for tens of thousands of years.

At first, the new planet was lifeless. But over the years chemicals formed. These joined together to form cells – single units of life which could reproduce themselves.

Simple plants, called algae, developed. These produced oxygen, which changed the atmosphere –

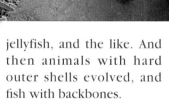

Each cell of blue-green algae produces oxygen. This makes the atmosphere breathable and supports life.

the gases that surround the planet. By 500 million years ago, the earth's air had become breathable.

THE FIRST ANIMALS

Sea creatures with soft bodies developed, which were made up of more than one cell - sponges, jellyfish, and the like. And then animals with hard outer shells evolved, and fish with backbones.

Some bony sea animals began to creep onto dry land, and eventually they developed legs and lungs for breathing. We call these creatures amphibians. Like frogs, they had to lay their eggs in water – so animals still had to evolve which could really take over the land.

THE AGE OF REPTILES

Each living thing is slightly different from others of the same species. When animals breed, they tend to develop the characteristics which help their chances of survival.

That is how, in time, new species develop. And that was how, over 300 million years ago, some amphibians changed into a new group of animals, called reptiles, which could lay their eggs on dry land.

Reptiles were so successful that they overran the planet. They developed into turtles, snakes, lizards, and gigantic crocodiles. The strongest were the dinosaurs.

The first creatures on Earth crawled out of the seas. They evolved into many different creatures including the dinosaurs.

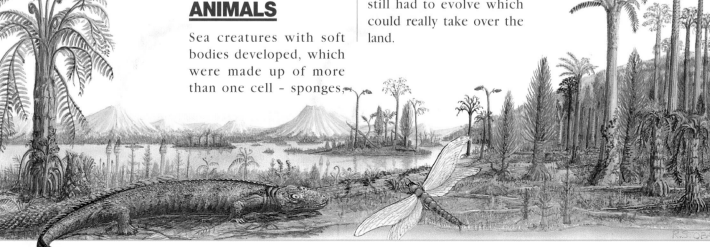

A WORLD RULED BUT FOR

How do scientists know what Earth was like in prehistoric times? They examine ancient rocks. Prehistoric plants and animals left behind marks and traces which later turned into stone, becoming fossils.

The fossil record tells scientists that at different periods the living conditions on Earth have changed. Each prehistoric period has been given its own name.

Dinosaurs laid eggs like modern reptiles and birds. Sometimes, fossilized eggs have been found.

JOURNEY TO THE JURASSIC

The dinosaur story begins in the Triassic period, between 225 and 193 million years ago, when the earth was hot and dry. In the Jurassic period, between 193 and 136 million years ago, the climate turned warm and wet, and the vegetation became lusher. Dinosaurs munched on swamp plants. Conditions on Earth changed yet again, and during the Cretaceous period (between 144 and 65 million years ago), flowering plants appeared on Earth for the first time. Dinosaurs thrived.

DINOSAUR DYNASTIES

Dinosaurs were all scaly reptiles, but they came in very different shapes and sizes. There were slow, lumbering giants such as *Brachiosaurus*, which weighed nearly 88 tons and *Diplodocus*, which had a 26-foot (8-m) long neck.

But other dinosaurs were much smaller. Compsognathus was only 24 inches (60 cm) long and weighed just 7 pounds (3 kg).

TOOTH AND CLAW

Some dinosaurs were peaceful plant eaters, grazing mosses and ferns in herds. Others were some of the most ferocious hunting animals the earth has ever seen. *Tyrannosaurus rex* was a fearsome flesh eater, its massive jaws lined with razor-sharp fangs. It was 49 feet (15 m) long. *Deinonychus* had great slashing claws on both its hands and feet.

Dinosaurs needed defenses against attack. Many had armor-plated hides, spiked or studded

Tyrannosaurus rex was a fierce hunter. It had a huge head which was 5 feet (1.5 m) long and razor-sharp teeth which were about 7 inches (18 cm) long.

BY REPTILES – HOW LONG?

Flying dinosaurs called pterosaurs ruled the skies. They had a wingspan of about 23 feet (7 m).

tails, and outlandish horns. *Triceratops* had three horns – two on the top of its head and one on the end of its nose! Some ostrich-like dinosaurs found safety in speed, running from danger on long, powerful legs.

FAMILY LIVING

As reptiles, dinosaurs laid eggs – just like today's crocodiles or snakes. Their eggs have survived as fossils, some still in the nest or even in the process of hatching out. Many baby dinosaurs would have grown up like today's wild animals, running with the herd or following their parents.

HOT OR COLD?

Other questions about dinosaurs remain unsolved. One crucial question is that of body heat. Some dinosaurs, such as *Stegosaurus*, had bony plates sticking up along its back, which probably helped to control its temperature. But were most dinosaurs warm-blooded or cold-blooded?

Today's reptiles are cold-blooded, which means that they warm their bodies by basking in the sun. Birds and mammals, on the other hand, are warm-blooded, with bodies that burn up food to make heat. And dinosaurs? Scientists are still arguing about the evidence.

THE END OF THE DAY?

Dinosaurs ruled the planet for millions of years. They included some of the most amazing creatures ever to have walked on Earth, and have to be rated as successful survivors.

So why is it there are no dinosaurs alive today? What made them extinct? Was there a sudden cataclysmic disaster? If so, why did it destroy one group of animals, but not others? Was all life on Earth under threat? ***What did happen to the world at the end of the Cretaceous period?***

Apatosaurus was a huge, plant-eating dinosaur. Its long neck enabled it to eat leaves and twigs from high in the branches, which other animals would not have been able to reach.

the climate. An explosion of this size would have blocked out sunlight, preventing cold-blooded animals from taking in warmth. Plants used for food would have died off, so that animals starved to death.

A bitterly cold period might then have been followed by rapid warming, as clouds of water vapor rose, blanketing the planet. Many creatures may have died in the heat.

The dinosaurs, and their reptilian relatives, the long-necked plesiosaurs and the flying pterosaurs, might never have recovered from such a global disaster. Only other animals, better able to cope with such great changes, may have been able to survive.

Meteorites are huge lumps of rock and ice that sometimes crash through the atmosphere to Earth. This is an artist's impression of how it might look.

WHAT HAPPENED NEXT?

WERE THE DINOSAURS POISONED?

Pollution threatens the survival of many species in our modern world, but this is usually caused by humans. But there were no humans alive at the time of the dinosaurs to poison the atmosphere. Long periods of volcanic activity may have filled the air with poisonous, sulfurous fumes, it is true. But surely volcanoes cannot have poisoned the whole planet, and if they had, would they not have killed off the mammals and amphibians, as well as the reptiles?

DID THE WEATHER CHANGE?

Perhaps the extinction of the dinosaurs took millions of years and was not the result of one sudden disaster. Changes to the world's climate happen very slowly, but they can have a dramatic effect on animal life. If the steady, warm climate became more variable, as it is today, dinosaurs would have been at a disadvantage - especially if they were cold-blooded. They would have been unable to cope with sudden periods of cold. Warm-blooded creatures, such as mammals, would have had no problem adapting to such a change of conditions.

A change in the weather could have led to changes in vegetation. But would all the dinosaurs die if the plants changed?

WAS THE EARTH HIT BY A METEORITE?

What kind of disaster might have brought the age of the dinosaurs to an end? Meteorites, lumps of rock that fly through space, sometimes collide with planets. A really huge meteorite might have done just this about 65 million years ago.

What would have been the result? A dense cloud of debris and dust would have risen, circling the globe. We know from studying the effect of modern volcanic eruptions that this would have caused major changes to

even hatched, the dinosaurs would have had no chance of survival.

When dinosaurs began to die out, mammals could have taken over their territory, evolving into larger species. The new prehistoric age, called the Cenozoic (meaning "new life") era by scientists, certainly saw mammals take over the earth. Mammals still rule the planet today, especially one species which appeared in recent times – the human being.

The first mammals were probably shrew-like creatures.

For 160 million years, dinosaurs ruled the planet.

They lived on the land, in the water and in the skies. They covered a range of shapes and sizes. What could possibly have happened to destroy these animals?

CAN YOU DECIDE THE FATE OF THE DINOSAURS?

DID THE MAMMALS TAKE OVER?

By the end of the Cretaceous period, new kinds of animals had evolved on Earth. Feathered birds now ruled the sky in place of the flying reptiles, while much of the land was taken over by mammals. The first mammals were small, furry animals that could hardly have challenged the larger, fiercer dinosaurs. But plagues of small mammals, or perhaps hungry birds and snakes, may have robbed dinosaur nests of their eggs. With their young being killed before they

Other sources of poison may have caused the dinosaurs to die off in large numbers. Many new kinds of plants had appeared on the planet for the first time during the Cretaceous period. Could it be that some or all of these were poisonous to dinosaurs and certain other animals? Did only the creatures that could eat these plants, or those that could find enough other plants to eat, survive?

But not all dinosaurs ate plants. Surely the poisonous plants would only kill those animals which ate them? That is true, but the flesh-eating dinosaurs ate plant-eating animals, and without plant-eating animals, these dinosaurs would also have died. So all the animals would have relied on a supply of healthy plant food.

Was there a huge volcanic explosion that wiped out the dinosaurs? Pollution in the atmosphere could have caused a change in the climate. Would this have led to the death of all these animals?

WHAT REALLY HAPPENED TO THE DINOSAURS?

Huge lumps of rock do sometimes fall from the sky. This meteorite was found in the Antarctic in 1981.

There was a disaster, for the dinosaurs at least, at the end of the Cretaceous period. It seems to have been very sudden, but then we are thinking in terms of such a vast time scale that this may be no single catastrophe lasting a few years.

ROCKS FROM SPACE

There can be little doubt that meteorites are capable of delivering terrible destruction to our planet. A 6-mile (10-km) wide rock traveling at 55,890 miles per hour (90,000 kph) would explode on Earth's surface with the same force as a huge number of nuclear bombs. And traces of rare minerals often found in meteorites have

Changes in the weather could have led to an ice age. The dinosaurs would not survive in the cold.

When meteorites hit the ground they can cause huge crates, such as this one in Arizona.

been discovered in 65-million-year-old rock. So it is just possible that the dinosaurs' downfall started in outer space.

ADAPTING TO CHANGE

A change of vegetation might well have forced the dinosaurs to starve, although it was probably not in particular poisonous plants that caused the problem.

The most likely reason for the extinction of the dinosaurs is a general change in climate and habitat. The question of whether dinosaurs were warm-blooded or cold-blooded is clearly very important here.

The mammals were obviously better suited to the new conditions. They were unlikely to have destroyed so many reptiles just by egg stealing, but they did benefit from the dinosaurs' disappearance.

LIVING RELATIVES

Birds are very like dinosaurs in many ways, and they share common ancestors. So the dinosaurs do have some relatives left on Earth today.

UNSOLVED MYSTERY

There is no single answer to the extinction puzzle. The 65-million-year-old mystery remains unsolved. But one thing should be made clear; dinosaurs have become a byword for creatures that cannot adapt to change. However, the fact is that they ruled the world for 150 million years. And that makes the whole of human history so far look like a brief footnote!

Scientists can learn about the lives of the dinosaurs by studying their fossilized bones.

THE SHADOW OF THE MOUNTAIN

After several unsettled years, following the bloodthirsty reign of the emperor Nero, life is returning to its peaceful, normal pace. The emperor Vespasian has soothed and strengthened the empire, and he has decided that his own son, Titus, will become the next emperor, following Vespasian's own death.

Roman emperors had gold coins made with their picture on it.

Pompeii was a wealthy city. Some of the rich inhabitants could afford gold oil lamps to light their homes.

The land around Pompeii was rich and fertile. Many farmers grew olives and grapes.

GENEROUS AND FAIR

Titus has fought against the Jewish rebels and thus has proved himself a worthy leader. He will be an ideal emperor as he is generous and fair. He will surely rule the empire with great skill and allow the peaceful people to continue their daily lives.

Roman emperors are seen as gods by the people. With each new emperor, every city declares its allegiance, and every year priests hold special services in praise of their emperor.

Rome is prospering and many villages have grown to be the size of cities. Pompeii is such a city. It was originally built in the sixth century B.C., and has grown considerably since then. Its fortunes have increased, and today, in the year A.D. 79, it is a thriving place to live.

SURVIVING AN EARTHQUAKE

It has survived sieges and, on February 5, A.D. 62, an earthquake, which left many buildings in ruins.

Pompeii is lucky, as Rome has given it much independence. Councils and magistrates have been appointed to preside over the running of the city, supervising the police and markets, and organizing road maintenance.

THE HEART OF THE CITY

The forum is the heart of the city where religious, political, and commercial matters are settled. Weights and measures are kept at the *mensa ponderraria*, or office of weights and measures, and are used to ensure that everyone gets a fair deal, when buying things at the markets.

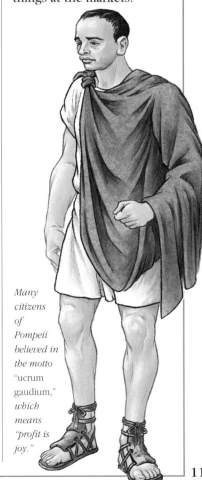

Many citizens of Pompeii believed in the motto "ucrum gaudium," which means "profit is joy."

11

Gladiators were highly respected in Roman culture. Many portraits were painted of them, such as this one on gilded glass.

Most Romans enjoy being entertained, therefore the theater is an important building in the city of Pompeii. There is also a large amphitheater for religious and athletic activities. Contests and games are held regularly with the aim of getting the highest number of pairs of gladiators to fight over a four- or five-day period.

Gladiators train at special combat schools, and their fighting is considered highly entertaining. But this is not the only spectacle held at the amphitheater. Gladiators might also fight lions, or spectators can watch lions as they fight each other or hunt domesticated animals.

THE CENTRAL BATHS

But probably the most important building in any Roman city is the baths. These are essential for daily life, and Pompeii has three public bathhouses. The newest and grandest is the Central Baths, which has not yet opened as its construction is only now nearing completion.

A GOOD LIFE

For most people, life in Pompeii is good. The fertile land on the mountain Vesuvius means that many crops can be grown including grapes for wine, olives for oil, as well as cereals and vegetables. Pompeii is also famous for its honey, which is used to sweeten the local wines, as well as for its onions and herbs, which are known throughout Rome to be particularly flavorsome.

Small shops sell freshly baked bread and delicately flavored cakes. Garum, a sauce much favored in Roman cooking, was also made in Pompeii, with freshly caught fish such as tuna or mackerel for a

The people of Pompeii enjoyed a high standard of living.

RAINED STONES

The Pompeiians believe in the good life – enjoying fine wines and good food. They celebrate their good fortune in their mosaics.

delicate flavor, or anchovies if the sauce was for the slaves.

THE WOOL AND METAL TRADES

Sheep breeding was common and supplied a flourishing wool trade, and Pompeii had a large number of skilled metal workers.

Following the earthquake, many people were employed rebuilding the city, and the profitable export trade increased. Wine and garum were sent as far away as Gaul, and wealthy landowners sold their surplus vegetables in the markets. Pompeian traders traveled far and wide selling their goods in such countries as Egypt, Africa, and Asia.

DAILY LIFE

The city is bustling with life, as the top gladiators are to fight in the amphitheater today. Also on the program are chariot races - a fast and furious sport.

The taverns are noisy with people enjoying a meal and a chance to hear the latest gossip. But the air in the streets is hot and heavy, and

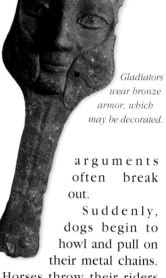

Gladiators wear bronze armor, which may be decorated.

arguments often break out.

Suddenly, dogs begin to howl and pull on their metal chains. Horses throw their riders and bolt away. Even wild birds seem to catch the fear and fly in frantic circles. The sky blackens. *A huge roar is heard, and a shower of burning stones rains down on the city.... What will happen to the people of Pompeii?*

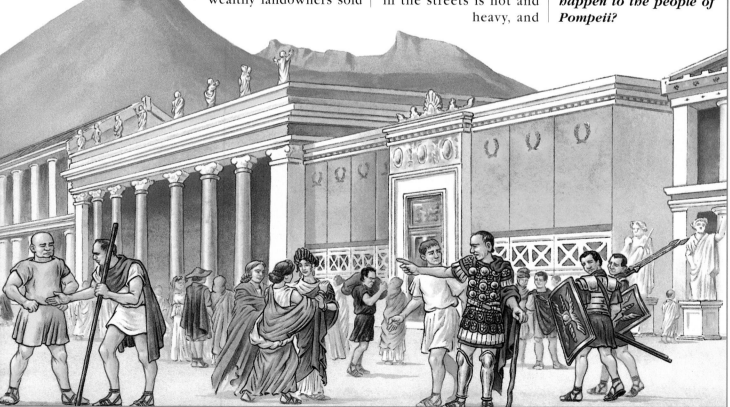

All Romans believed that the emperor was a god. What if the other gods decided to punish the emperor by destroying them?

WAS IT AN EARTHQUAKE?

On 5 February AD 62, an earthquake had destroyed much of the town. Was this another one? The earthquake had wiped out many villages and much of the city of Herculaneum as well as destroying many buildings in Pompeii.

Flocks of sheep grazing in the fields had disappeared and statues had been cracked. Many buildings had be restored and even more new ones had been built to replace them – had all this hard work been in vain if another earthquake was just going to shake their world again?

WHAT HAPPENED NEXT?

A dormant volcano looks very like any other mountain. Was it possible that their mountain was a volcano?

WAS IT DIVINE RETRIBUTION FOR THE ACTS OF THE EMPEROR?

Was god punishing them for the acts of their emperor? Rumours were circulating around the Jewish communities that god was seeking revenge for the terrible acts committed against the Jews by Titus – particularly when he had captured Jerusalem from the Jewish rebels and destroyed the Temple eight years previously. All Romans believed their emperor to

be a god and worshipped him accordingly. Special shrines were built, dedicated to the emperor, and games and services were held in his honour. Certainly the people of Pompeii revered the emperor Titus as their god. Had the other gods decided that the emperor was wrong? Was this the other gods way of punishing him by hurting them?

14

Before the earthquake, many animals had behaved strangely, horses had bolted, and dogs had fled. Was this another earthquake?

HAD ATLAS STUMBLED?

The Romans believed that the god Atlas supported the world on his shoulders. He was being punished for warring against the god Zeus, and had to support the world on his shoulders for all eternity. What would happen if he stumbled? Would he drop the whole world?

And if he did drop the world, what then? Would it fall forever? Surely the other gods would not allow the world to fall? The Romans worshipped many gods, surely one of them would save them?

The Romans believed that Atlas was condemned for all time to support the world. What would happen if he stumbled?

The people of Pompeii were enjoying a bountiful life.
What was making all the animals so restless? The air was certainly hot and heavy. Was a storm brewing? Or was it something else?

CAN YOU DECIDE THE FATE OF THE PEOPLE OF POMPEII?

WAS IT A VOLCANO ?

Pompeii was built in the shadow of the mountain called Vesuvius. This mountain dominated the skyline and provided the local people with richly fertile soil on its slopes in which they grew their crops. It was because of the good soil that the people were able to grow such good crops, and so become wealthy. Was it possible that this mountain was, in fact, a volcano that had been lying dormant for centuries? There was no way of telling if the mountain would explode, as there was no record of it ever having done so in the past.

WHAT REALLY HAPPENED AT POMPEII?

The volcano, Vesuvius, erupts, showering Pompeii in deadly ash.

Vesuvius, the mountain, was indeed a volcano and had erupted. Burning pumice and hot ash rained down on Pompeii and also on the city of Herculaneum. People everywhere ran for their lives. Some escaped to the bay, where they were horrified to see the sea retreating, leaving fish and other sea animals writhing in the mud.

The ruined amphitheatre shows the wealth of the people before their destruction.

RAINING FIRE

As the burning lava fell on the entire city, buildings caught fire. Huge rocks were hurled into the sky by the full force of the explosion falling and destroying anything that they landed on. Panic ensued as people rushed to get away from the burning city.

Everything around was covered in a thick layer of smoldering ash, in some places the ash was knee-deep in just a matter of minutes. Huge clouds of poisonous, foul-smelling gas belched from the volcano, flooring people as they fled.

FROZEN IN TIME

Over 2,000 people died when Vesuvius erupted on August 24, A.D. 79. Many suffocated in the poisonous fumes and were buried beneath the falling ash and pumice, which then covered their bodies.

The surprise of the eruption is shown by the fact that most of the people were going about their normal daily business.

Bakers were discovered, with bread still in the ovens, and many people were buried where they fell, running through the streets.

The town was virtually forgotten until the middle of the eighteenth century when archaeologists uncovered it. They found a complete record of daily life in Roman times frozen in time.

People were encased in the falling ash as they tried to escape. The shape of their bodies is preserved for all time.

Many buildings and mosaics have survived virtually intact.

"BRING OUT YOUR DEAD"

It's the beginning of summer, and travel is easy. Crusades and fairs are part of everyday life. Strange countries with different customs are visited, and stories of fighting the Saracens abound.

Towns are changing. There are more houses but fewer orchards and vineyards. Horses jostle through the streets, while cats and dogs forage for scraps. Everyone is careful where they walk - butchers slaughter animals outside their shops and throw the blood into the street. Sewers run down the middle of the narrow streets, so in hot weather the smell is unbearable.

Crusaders believed they were soldiers of Christ and fought to reclaim the Holy Lands from the Muslims.

MARKET DAY

Certain days are set aside for markets and fairs. Merchants from all over Europe gather to celebrate and trade - woolen cloth from western Europe is traded for spices. Luxury goods can be bought cheaply or bartered for fine wines, olives, and fruit.

Every July, the Hot Fair is held in the Champagne region of France. Traders come from Italy, Germany, Spain, England, Flanders and further away.

Rich merchants and their wives would travel for miles to reach the country fairs.

SPICES AND SILKS

At the fairground, sacks and bales of precious goods are unloaded from ponies and carts - luxury goods of every description - silks, spices, pearls, metals, furs, ivory, and rich woolen cloth. Sugar, salt, and dyes - particularly those that color cloth red - are much prized.

Many different products were traded at the fairs. Here, meat and game are being cut up and sold.

Saffron is worth more than its weight in gold. Pepper is hugely popular and is sold by the peppercorn - housewives can buy just one. Everyone tries to get the best deal, and the bargaining is fierce. There are even courts to settle major disputes.

The streets are bustling. Acrobats, dancing bears, and jugglers perform at street corners, as the local people mix with strangers from faraway places.

"WHAT IS THIS

People carried posies of sweet-smelling herbs and flowers to protect them from the "bad air," which they thought made them sick.

After the fair, life returns to normal. The merchants gather their unsold wares and continue their journeys, either returning home, or traveling on to the next fair.

All the houses look similar, but the rich occupy whole buildings, not just one or two rooms. The houses are also home to many unwelcome visitors - mice, rats, fleas, bedbugs, and other insects are common.

HERBS FOR HEALING

All food is cooked over an open fire, and most meals consist of broths or thick soups, stews, and roast meats. Women grow herbs, both to flavor the food and for medicinal use. The herbs are usually boiled in water, and the liquid is either served as a drink or used as a lotion. Garlic is used to cure infections, sage can be used to bring down swellings, and rue helps digestion and is said to cure poisoning.

CURES FOR THE RICH?

Doctors are expensive, and their cures often do more harm than good. They think that medicine is linked to magic, and that the body has four "humours" and three "spirits," all of which can be examined by looking at urine and stools. Recovery depends on many things, including the position of the stars and the moon.

Leeches are a favorite cure, as doctors believe that most illnesses are caused by bad blood. They believe that

After examining a patient, a doctor may prescribe a medicine made from herbs.

by removing the bad blood, the patient will get better.

Diseases, like typhoid and pneumonia are very common, and doctors do their best to help the sick. Leprosy is widespread, and there is no known cure. Lepers are feared and made to clack castanets or ring a bell to announce their presence wherever they go. Many are sent to live in special colonies away from healthy people. Others were not so lucky. In France in 1313, Philip the Fair gave orders for all lepers to be burned.

With sickness everywhere, people thought their food might be poisoned. Some people preferred to eat dried meat, rather than fresh.

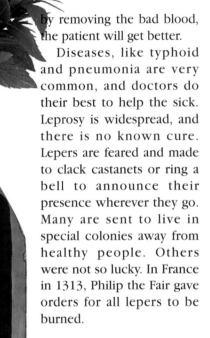

STRANGE ILLNESS?'

Neither prayer nor medicine seemed to help against this strange illness.

RELEASING EVIL SPIRITS

Doctors also treat the mentally ill. Trepanning, the practice of drilling a hole into a living patient's skull to release the evil spirits, is still the most common way to treat bad headaches.

A NEW SICKNESS

But a new illness, against which the doctors know no cure, is spreading through the towns and cities of Europe. An illness so strange and so deadly has not been seen before. Symptoms start with shivering, and then red rings develop on the skin. Next comes a fever, with sneezing and coughing up blood. Dizziness and seeing strange things that aren't there follow. Then painful blue swellings appear under the arms and in the groin. The body turns black, and death quickly follows. The whole illness usually lasts just three days, and people have given it a name - the black death, as nothing can save them.

Doctors cannot stop this unseen killer. Rich and poor suffer together. Doctors try to protect themselves by wearing masks with glass eyes and a long nose, stuffed with perfume. Ordinary people carry posies of scented herbs and flowers to make sure they are breathing clean, sweet-smelling air, or soak their clothes in sweet vinegar to wash away the germs.

SPELLS AND MAGIC

Children and their parents chant rhymes to protect themselves. Magic talismans and spells are sold at street corners - "Abracadabra" written in a triangle is said to be a powerful enough charm to ward off this unknown illness.

LORD HAVE MERCY

Whole houses are sealed when the illness is found. For 40 days and 40 nights no one is allowed out of a house where someone is sick. A cross is painted on the door together with the words "Lord have mercy on us." The healthy and the sick can only wait....

With so many people dying, burials take place at night. The only sound along the deserted streets is that of a bell and the cry *"Bring out your dead."*

Doctors used leeches to suck out the bad blood, but this had no effect against this deadly new disease.

Carts carry the dead out beyond the city limits, where gravediggers dig huge pits in which young and old, rich and poor are buried together. *Will everyone die of this unknown illness? Can nothing be done to save them?*

WAS IT GOD'S PUNISHMENT?

Had the whole world become so evil that God could see no hope but to wipe out all the living and start again? True, people had become more vain – women wore cosmetics and wigs. The feminine ideal was said to be a slender figure with blonde hair and fair skin. Some women used ointments to lighten their skin, but more often than not these took the skin off along with the coloring. Preachers warned that the Virgin Mary would never have worn silken belts interwoven with gold and silver. But would God really send so violent a punishment to everyone and not just the vain young women? Surely God could not doubt their devotion when so many went on Crusades to fight the Holy Wars?

Preachers warned that God would punish those who were so vain. Some people were so frightened by this that they punished themselves – even whipping themselves to show God how sorry they were.

Doctors wore long gowns and masks. They examined people with long-handled instruments.

WHAT HAPPENED NEXT?

WAS IT CAUSED BY ANIMALS?

Could animals get the sickness, and if so, were they spreading it to people? Cats, dogs, pigs, and even wolves scavenged for food in the streets among all the trash – maybe they were the cause?

But maybe it was something smaller? What about the rats? They got into everything – including the houses. What if they carried the disease?

Perhaps it was something even smaller still? The rats themselves often had fleas on their backs, and these could live in the houses just as easily as the rats did. Maybe they were causing the sickness? Or maybe it was something so tiny that it couldn't be seen by the eye – something so small that even the fleas could carry it?

The kitchen was often the center of activity in a house. Food was prepared and cooked over large fires, while other people made butter or passed the time of day with neighbors.

WAS IT CAUSED BY POOR MEDICINE?

Doctors studied the medical knowledge of the Greeks and Romans, and monks brought information from the Arabs. But were they right? None of the usual cures, such as bloodletting, helped the sick. Maybe the medicine was part of the problem? Maybe the doctors weren't helping at all; perhaps they were making things worse? Despite their efforts to protect themselves, many have fallen sick and died. If their treatments don't even work on themselves, whom will they work on?

A strange and terrible illness was sweeping the country, against which there was no cure.

What was causing the sickness? Would everyone die before a cure could be found? Fear was also spreading as no one knew what was making people sick.

CAN YOU DISCOVER WHAT CAUSED THIS ILLNESS?

Rats were pests in many houses. They were often infested with fleas.

WAS IT CAUSED BY BAD FOOD?

Was this dreadful illness caused by bad food? There were no refrigerators and food did spoil quickly. The techniques for keeping food fresh were limited. Fish might be kept alive in leather tanks in the kitchens, or they might be pickled in vinegar, smoked, or salted. Meat was also salted, while fruit, vegetables, and herbs were preserved by drying them in the sun. If the food was bad when it was eaten, could this cause the sickness?

Or was the sickness passed from person to person? Shopping for food became a new hazard. People stopped passing food from hand to hand, in case one person was carrying the sickenss, and coins were soaked in vinegar for hours to wash away any germs.

Or perhaps the water supply was contaminated? The sewers ran down the streets, so maybe the waste had seeped into the clean drinking water. In some places, people thought they were being deliberately poisoned. Many Europeans believed that the Jews were poisoning the wells. In Mainz, in Germany, over 12,000 Jews were foolishly burned because of this.

WHAT REALLY HAPPENED TO THE BLACK DEATH?

The illness was, in fact, bubonic plague. It continued to ravage the population of Europe for some 300 years, from 1348 until the end of the seventeenth century. During this time, the plague killed 25 million people – about one-third of the population at that time. Whole communities were wiped out – in 1386 in the Russian city of Smolensk, only five people survived the disease, and in London, the chances of survival were just one in ten.

The bacteria Yersinia pestis *causes bubonic plague. Fleas infected with the bacteria were carried by rats or possibly brought to trade fairs in rolls of woolen cloth.*

The plague continued to kill large numbers of the population until the end of the 17th century.

A TINY BACTERIA

Bubonic plague is caused by a bacteria called *Yersinia pestis*. This is carried by fleas, which in turn are carried by rats.

The fleas spread the disease when they feed on a rat or a person.

KILL OR CURE?

In the fourteenth century, no one knew how to control the disease. Doctors tried several new remedies, many of which probably killed the patients instead of curing them! In some cases, doctors cut open the boils and inserted red-hot pokers in an attempt to clean the wound. Doctors did not have anesthetics, and the terrified patient often died of shock or had a heart attack.

IMPROVED HYGIENE

The most effective way to prevent the spread of the disease was to improve hygiene. As people began to clean their houses and themselves more thoroughly, the bacteria had less chance of survival.

But the plague bacteria has not been completely eradicated. In some parts of the world, there may still be more than 100 reported cases of plague per million of the population. However, with correct diagnosis, bubonic plague is curable, as it can be treated successfully with antibiotics.

Modern antibiotics are effective in treating bubonic plague. Although the disease still exists today, its spread can be controlled.

THE MILLIONAIRE'S SPECIAL

Travel across the Atlantic has never been so good. True, it is still a formidable ocean, but modern ships can overcome the perils and more and more passengers are crossing from Great Britain to start new lives in the United States of America.

The Titanic *was built at the Harland & Wolff shipyard in Belfast, Ireland.*

THE POWER OF STEAM

When the first passenger ships crossed the Atlantic in the 1750s, the journey took nearly 28 days. But later, in the mid-1840s, Isambard Kingdom Brunel's ship *Great Britain* completed the journey in just 14 days and 21 hours. Described by the *New York Herald* as "a monster from the deep," this remarkable ship can cover a distance of 160 miles (258 km) a day using full engines.

TRAVELING IN STYLE

Comfort is just as important as speed as most of the big companies know. Certainly, The White Star Line, which was founded by Thomas Ismay, recognized this. The *Oceanic,* which came into service in 1899, was the height of luxury with huge cabins equipped with bathrooms with freshwater taps and electric bells to summon the stewards.

THE WAY FORWARD

One evening in 1907, J. Bruce Ismay, who inherited control of the White Star Line in 1900 following the death of his father, was dining with his old friend William James Pirrie, a partner in the shipbuilding firm Harland & Wolff. Together, over coffee and cigars, they devised a plan to build three ships of such sumptuous luxury that transatlantic passengers would refuse to travel on any other ships. Their ships will be called the *Olympic,* *Titanic,* and *Britannic.*

The Titanic *is towed away from the shipyards, ready for her maiden voyage from Southampton, Great Britain, to New York.*

William J. Pirrie and his partner J. Bruce Ismay planned to build three luxurious ships for transatlantic travel.

The Great Britain*'s steam engines dramatically reduced journey times across the Atlantic.*

LUXURY TRIPS
ATLANTIC BY

No expense is to be spared in the building and equipping of these ships. Attention to comfort and detail is everything. So what if there is no dock large enough for these goliaths, nor any shipyard big enough to build them – Ismay and Pirrie are undeterred. Harland & Wolff in Belfast, Ireland, will construct specially strengthened slipways to bear the weight of these huge ships.

A wireless operator takes messages in the radio room.

A GRAND SCALE

Everything about these ships is on an extravagant scale. The *Titanic*'s four funnels are so huge that each one is large enough to drive two trains through, and each of the three propellers is as big as a windmill.

Housed within the ship's eight decks are accommodation's for 3,547 people – 905 in first class, 564 in second, and 1,134 in third. The remaining 944 are for the crew.

Detailed discussions are held to plan every feature. In one such meeting, they discussed decoration for five hours, leaving just ten minutes to discuss the number of lifeboats. Ismay and Pirrie decided they needed an extra four, in addition to those required by law.

SAFETY FIRST

The *Titanic* will have an iron hull. It will also have a double bottom. The outer skin of iron will be one inch (2.5 cm) thick. Even if this is pierced, an inner skin, also of iron, will keep the water out.

The splendor of the ship is remarkable. A huge foyer with a wrought iron glass dome covering was built over the first class stairway. And the *Titanic* is one of the first ocean liners to have its own swimming pool and squash courts.

Captain Smith was the senior captain with the White Star Line. He was chosen to sail the Titanic *on her maiden voyage.*

The Titanic *sailed from Southampton for New York in April 1912.*

ATLANTIC OCEAN

ACROSS THE STEAMSHIP

A sweeping stairway led into a large foyer. Passenger comfort was of prime importance and everything about the ship was on a grand scale.

LUXURY AND WEALTH

Nicknamed "Millionaire's Special," the *Titanic* will make its maiden voyage from Southampton to New York City on Wednesday, April 10, 1912. Edward J. Smith has been chosen as captain. This will be his final voyage as he will retire from the White Star Line after 38 years of service.

Many famous people are among the passengers making this trip. Colonel John Jacob Astor, reportedly the richest man in the world, is on board with his young wife, together with Mr. and Mrs. Straus, who founded Macy's - the world's largest department store. Mr. J. Bruce Ismay is also on board, representing the White Star Line, but ill health has prevented his partner, William Pirrie, from making the trip.

The radio operators are busy - people think it is fun to send messages to friends from the middle of the ocean.

Iceberg warnings are received, but that's not unusual - icebergs are fairly common in April, and anyway, everyone knows the *Titanic* is unsinkable.

In the crow's nest, Fred Fleet is waiting to be relieved from his watch duty. It's 11:40 p.m. and he is watching the calm, dark blue sea. Suddenly, a huge shadowy shape looms up, and the order is given to reverse engines. *A sickening crunch is heard and then silence... even the engines have stopped running...*

WHAT HAPPENED NEXT?

DID THE *TITANIC* HIT A WHALE?

Had the *Titanic* hit something - possibly a whale? Both blue whales and sperm whales are not uncommon in the Atlantic, even this far north. Blue whales can grow up to 100 feet (31 m) long and sperm whales up to 60 feet (18 m). The *Titanic* itself was over 880 feet (268 m) long. Could the *Titanic* have bumped into one of these magnificent creatures in the darkness - and if so, how much damage could a whale do to a ship of this size? Even if it did damage the hull, the designers had built in a reinforced bottom, which meant that no water could get in.

Whales do not usually travel alone - maybe it had hit a whole school, before Fred Fleet could warn the captain

COULD THEY HAVE HIT A SUBMARINE?

Military forces were said to be testing secret weapons in the area. Maybe they were testing submarines as underwater weapons. Had the *Titanic* hit one of these?

Fred Fleet, the man on watch, would not have had a chance to see that in the darkness, particularly as he was trained to look out for dangers on top of the sea and not underneath it. But surely, if the navy was testing new weapons in the area, wouldn't they have warned the commercial ships to keep away? Perhaps the *Titanic* was off course and sailing into the navy's test area. Captain Smith was a very experienced sailor,

but he could have made a mistake with his calculations. Maybe the *Titanic* was miles off course and sailing away from America instead of toward it.

Submarines were already being tested in the Atlantic waters. Had the Titanic hit a submerged submarine while sailing across the water?

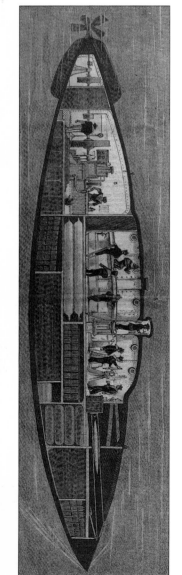

The radio room had received several iceberg warnings. Had the Titanic hit one?

HAD THE TITANIC HIT AN ICEBERG?

True enough, they had had several iceberg warnings th... day, but they were not uncommon for this time of ye... Surely the watch would have been able to see an icebe... before it got anywhere close – that's what they were there f... after all. And even if they had hit something, the reinforced h... would mean there was no danger. The *Titanic's* hull was divid... into a number of watertight compartments, and the passenge... had been told it would float if even four of these compartmen... were flooded. Even if it had hit something, with these very lat... safety features, what possible danger could they be in?

On the night of April 14, 1912, the *Titanic* suddenly stopped its engines.

Had the Titanic hit something or had the engines failed? What would happen to this huge ship that everyone said was unsinkable?

CAN YOU DECIDE WHAT HAPPENED TO THE *TITANIC?*

DID THE ENGINES FAIL?

Maybe the crunch had happened when the engines failed? Even on a ship as lavish as this, accidents could happen. Perhaps at any moment the captain would announce that one of the twenty-nine, 15-foot (5-m) high boilers had overheated, and they had shut off the engines as a precaution. Spending the rest of the night in the cold, still sea would be fine, as the *Titanic* was unsinkable. Surely by morning, the crew's engineers would have located the fault and have the ship running again. Who knows, maybe they could even make up some of the lost time and still arrive in New York on time.

With so much attention given to luxury, had enough thought been given to powering the ship? Perhaps the engines were not up to the job?

that they were there. At night it would be easy to miss their dark shapes swimming close to the surface.

Perhaps the captain had tried to reverse the engines to avoid the whales and had then decided to stop the propellers, so that they wouldn't get hurt as they swam underneath the huge ship. As soon as they had swum away, Captain Smith would give the order to restart the engines, and the journey would carry on as before.

Huge whales, such as the blue whale, are often found in the Atlantic. Had the Titanic *hit a whale?*

WHAT REALLY HAPPENED TO THE TITANIC?

The Titanic *hit an iceberg, which made a hole in its hull.*

I n the darkness, a huge iceberg crossed the path of the *Titanic*. Fred Fleet quickly sounded the alarm, and the engines were reversed. The iceberg struck a glancing blow along the *Titantic*'s starboard bow, covering the decks with several tons of ice.

which heard the *Titanic*'s distress calls and raced to its aid. But the remaining 1,522 people, including the ship's captain, drowned.

DISCOVERY

The wreck of the *Titanic* was discovered about 300 miles (480 km) off the coast of Newfoundland by Robert D. Ballard in September 1985. Using a robot submarine, he explored the wreck and discovered much about its fate. He also left a plaque at the site, dedicated to all those who died that night.

The lifeboats leave the sinking ship. The unthinkable had happened – the unsinkable ship could not live up to its name, and sank.

board. Some jumped into the icy water, while others huddled together at the stern.

SINKING

At 2:17 a.m. the water flooded the forward compartments, and the *Titanic* lurched forward. The ship could not take the strain of having its stern in the air and is thought to have snapped in two between the third and fourth funnels and sank.

Of the 2,227 passengers and crew aboard the ship that night, 705 escaped in the ship's 20 lifeboats and life rafts, including J. Bruce Ismay. Many were picked up by another ship, the *Carpathia*,

In 1985 the wreck of the Titanic *was discovered on the Atlantic seabed. Many of those who died that night were never found. Others were buried in this cemetery in Nova Scotia.*

WATER EVERYWHERE

Water was pouring in through the gaping hole in the *Titanic*'s hull. The divisions between the watertight compartments did not reach the ceiling, and water was overflowing from one to the next. The ship could stay afloat if four of these compartments flooded – but 20 minutes

after the accident, a fifth was already filling up.

At about 12:30 a.m. Captain Smith ordered people into the lifeboats - women and children first. But in spite of the extra safety precautions, there were not enough lifeboats for everyone on board.

By 2:00 a.m. all the lifeboats had left the stricken vessel, but over 1,500 people were still on

AIRSHIPS – TRANSPORT OF THE FUTURE?

The age of air travel is upon us. Vast airships have proved conclusively to be superior to their rivals, the hot-air balloons. Although spectacular in appearance, hot-air balloons have frustrating limitations – they are difficult to steer, and it is almost impossible to control their speed.

True, the development of the airship owes much to its competitor, the balloon. Ever since 1783, when the Montgolfier brothers first demonstrated that balloons filled with hot smoke could fly, the race has been on to find a way to control the flight.

Airships promised controlled flight and were increasingly popular. This French airship was called La France *and was tested in 1884.*

The Montgolfier brothers' balloon makes its first manned ascent.

LIGHTER THAN AIR

Hydrogen gas is known to be about fourteen times lighter than air, but it escapes too easily from the Montgolfier balloons. But J.A.C. Charles, a physicist, has developed a way of containing it. He paints a rubber solution inside the silk balloon, making it hydrogen-tight. And it floats perfectly.

KEEPING CONTROL

Now people are trying to find a way of controlling the aircraft. After years of unsuccessful attempts, Daimler has invented the gasoline engine, which is light, powerful, and reliable – everything an aeronaut could wish for.

In July 1900, Count Ferdinand von Zeppelin launched his first airship, *LZ1*. It was divided into segments using a sturdy aluminum frame, which meant it could be larger and have a greater range.

FOUNDING DELAG

In November 1909, with his new partner Hugo Eckener, Ferdinand von Zeppelin founded DELAG,

Deutsch Luftschiffahrts Aktien Gesellschaft (the German Airship Transport Company) and set up a network of airship routes for passengers between major German cities. By 1912 several airships were being used. This proved a remarkably safe way to travel – between 1912 and 1914, DELAG carried more than 10,000 passengers on nearly 1,590 flights without any mishaps.

Count Ferdinand von Zeppelin developed a larger airship that could fly longer distances.

Airships were a fairly common sight flying between airbases at Lakehurst, New Jersey, and Frankfurt in Germany.

After World War I, Eckener set his sights on a transatlantic crossing from Germany to the United States. In October 1928, the huge *Graf Zeppelin* took to the sky and successfully completed its first voyage.

When laden with cargo and a full complement of 20 paying passengers, *Graf Zeppelin* could cruise at about 70 miles (113 km) per hour. Eckener knew that this was too slow for rough weather and that to provide a reliable all-weather service, he needed a faster ship.

LUXURY AND SAFETY

By March 1936, a new airship was being developed – the *Hindenburg*. It was the epitome of style and engineering. At just over 800 feet (244 m) long, it could travel at a maximum speed of 84 mph (135 kph) when fully laden. The *Hindenburg* could complete the crossing in just under 65 hours.

Airships were designed for comfort and luxury. Travelers could relax in the lounge and observation car, while meals were served in the saloon.

HINDENBURG

MODERN LUXE

The *Hindenburg* was designed with luxury in mind. Each of the 25, two-berth cabins was heated and had hot and cold running water. And as a real luxury, the ship was equipped with its own bar and smoking room.

Despite being so close to all the hydrogen gas needed to keep the *Hindenburg* airborne, smoking was allowed in just this one place. A system of double doors kept all the smoke inside, and the only lighter on board was chained to the side in this room. Passengers had to surrender all matches and lighters to the captain on boarding the aircraft.

The airship's designers knew the danger of using hydrogen, and had wanted to use helium. But the United States was the only country that had this gas in any quantity, and they were wary of the German chancellor, Adolf Hitler. The Americans did not trust the Nazis and felt that they might use their airships for military purposes if they had access to helium.

The *Hindenburg* came into service in 1936. It flew between Lakehurst, New Jersey, in the United States and Frankfurt in Germany. On May 4, 1937, the *Hindenburg* left Frankfurt carrying 36 passengers and 61 crew, en route to Lakehurst. Storms were rumbling around the Lakehurst area, and Captain Max Pruss kept waiting for the bad weather to clear.

CLEAR TO LAND

At about 7:00 P.M., only light clouds remained, and the captain carefully steered the *Hindenberg* into position beside its landing mast. At 7:25 P.M., mooring ropes were thrown from the airship and caught by the ground crew. The engines were reversed for braking, and the radio operator reported to the *Graf Zeppelin* that the crossing had been successful. **Suddenly a huge flame shot out from the top of the Hindenburg.**

The Hindenburg *was supported by an aluminum frame. Her route took her across the Atlantic Ocean.*

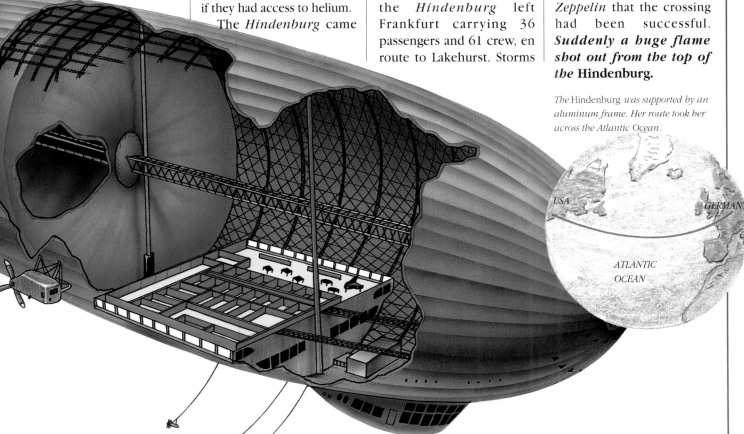

USA

GERMANY

ATLANTIC OCEAN

WAS THE EXPLOSION CAUSED BY A BUILD-UP OF STATIC ELECTRICITY?

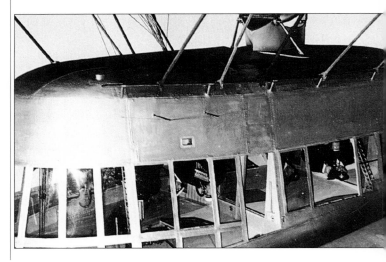

The captain controlled the airship from the flight deck, a construction beneath the canopy. Did he make a mistake and crash the airship?

The internal frame of the airship was made of aluminum and supported by stay wires. Suppose one of these wires had snapped and as it sprung back, pierced the skin of the airship. The swinging wire would have caused a buildup of static electricity, which could create a spark. The escaping hydrogen gas would mix with oxygen in the air and create a dangerous and highly flammable mixture. If the static electricity did cause a spark, this could easily have lit the hydrogen and air, causing a huge and terrible explosion.

Sparks can occur when static electricity builds up. Did such a spark cause the Hindenburg to burst into flames?

THE AIRSHIP *HINDENBURG*

WHAT HAPPENED NEXT?

WAS THE AIRSHIP HIT BY LIGHTNING?

Storms had surrounded the area and delayed the landing. Had Captain Pruss misjudged the weather and arrived just in time for another storm? The airships had proved that they could fly in all weather, and it was thought that they could sustain a direct hit by lightning as the metal framework would absorb the charge. But what if a small hole appeared in the balloon containing the hydrogen? Everyone knew that if hydrogen mixes with air and a flame, it will explode. Was this what had happened to the mighty *Hindenburg*?

DID THE PILOT CRASH?

Captain Max Pruss was an experienced pilot, but even so, he could have made a mistake. He had already delayed the landing as they were surrounded by thunderstorms. He may have been tired and decided to land without really taking into account the weather and conditions on the ground. The storms may suddenly have gusted, throwing the airship out of control. Ernst A. Lehmann was also on board the airship. He had captained the *Hindenburg* on several occasions. Even if Pruss made a bad judgment, surely between the two of them they would have had enough experience to tackle every situation.

Airships were becoming increasingly popular with international travelers.

They were luxurious and comfortable, and until now, safe. So why had flames shot out from the Hindenburg's balloon? What had caused the explosion?

CAN YOU DECIDE WHAT HAPPENED TO THE AIRSHIP?

The Nazi Party was gaining control in Germany, but they faced some opposition. Had someone fired a gun inside the airship, ripping a hole in the balloon and causing it to explode?

WAS IT SABOTAGED?

The Germans were becoming increasingly unpopular throughout the world, and many people feared the intentions of the chancellor, Adolf Hitler. The Nazi Party was gaining influence throughout Germany, and much of the rest of the world was concerned about this rise in power.

Hitler insisted that the airships fly under his flag, the swastika, and this may well have led someone to try to destroy it. One of the crew, a man named Erich Spehl, was regarded with suspicion by his fellow crewmen. He was known to have communist sympathies. He would certainly have had an opportunity to sabotage the ship if that had been his intention.

Lightning produces huge surges of electrical power. Did one such surge rip through the fabric of the Hindenburg's balloon and cause the hydrogen gas to explode?

WHAT REALLY HAPPENED TO THE HINDENBURG?

I n the control car, Max Pruss felt the airship jerk and saw below a red tinge reflected on the ground. He instantly realized that the ship was on fire and knew that he must land as quickly as possible. The huge airship burst into flames and dropped from the sky, showering onlookers and ground crew alike with sparks and flames.

The Hindenburg*'s sturdy aluminum frame can be seen clearly through the burning balloon.*

The huge airship exploded in a ball of flames as she approached the landing mast at Lakehurst.

Miraculously 63 people on board the Hindenburg *survived the explosion.*

Of the 97 passengers and crew who were aboard the *Hindenburg*, 35 died at Lakehurst, together with one member of the ground crew. Ernst Lehmann was one of them. He managed to stagger clear of the wreckage but died later in the hospital.

NO SINGLE ANSWER

No one knows for certain why the *Hindenburg* burst into flames, although there are several theories. Eckener favored the view that the stay wire snapping had pierced the skin and caused static electricity. Theories of sabotage abounded, particularly as a Luger pistol, from which one shot had been fired, was found in the wreckage. The only thing that all theories agreed upon, was that the accident could have been avoided if helium had been used to inflate the balloon.

OUT OF ACTION

Immediately after the disaster, the remaining airships were taken out of service. By September 1938 when *Graf Zeppelin II* was ready for service, the United States had hardened its attitude toward Germany. Adolf Hitler was in power, and the promised helium was never delivered. Despite successful test flights using hydrogen, the airship was doomed since public confidence was destroyed.

The remaining airships were broken up soon after the war started, and their aluminum frames used for the Luftwaffe. A new mode of transport completely overshadowed the airship – the airplane.

A RUDE AWAKENING

The planet Earth is a giant ball of rock spinning in space. At its center, the temperature is an incredible 10,832°F (6000°C). The core of the planet is made of iron, but around this core are layers of molten and semimolten metals. The next layer, or mantle, supports the planet's surface, the hard crust on which we live.

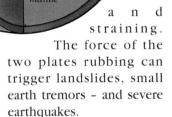

In cross-section, the Earth would have four main layers. Only the crust is really solid. The inner layers of the Earth are very hot in temperature.

inner core

outer core

mantle

crust

CORE TO CRUST

The rocks of the Earth's crust are very thin – between 19 and 43 miles (30 and 70 km) on land, as little as 4 to 6 miles (6-10 km) beneath the sea. Not surprisingly, the crust has cracked in places. The cracked sections, called plates, float on beds of molten rock called magma.

SHIFTING GROUND

The heat from the center of the Earth makes the plates move. In fact, over many millions of years, whole land masses have moved, or drifted, around the world's surface. We don't normally notice these movements because they

When volcanoes erupt, molten rock, called magma, is forced out from inside the Earth.

are very, very slow.

When two plates collide, one of them may be pushed down into the magma, where the intense heat causes it to melt. New magma may then be

forced upward through any weak parts of the crust, bursting out in volcanic eruptions.

Sometimes the edge of one plate meets the edge of another one along a great crack, or fault. The two edges rub together, shifting

and straining.

The force of the two plates rubbing can trigger landslides, small earth tremors – and severe earthquakes.

THE PACIFIC CRUNCH

One great crack, called the San Andreas Fault, runs down the western coast of the United States. It marks the boundaries of the Pacific Plate and the North American Plate.

The Pacific Plate is moving in a northwesterly direction. The speed of the shift, which is about 2 inches (5 cm) a year, may not seem to be that fast. But it is critical. The stresses and strains it sets off in the rocks make this is one of the world's worst earthquake zones. And some of United States's biggest cities, including Los Angeles and San Francisco, are built on the edge of the Pacific Plate.

The surface or crust of the Earth forms solid plates which float on the molten layers below. This map shows where the plates join.

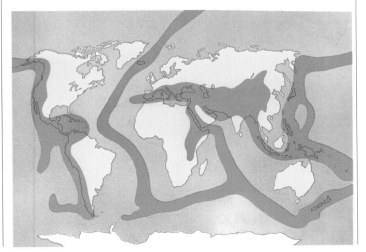

SAN FRANCISCO TIME

One of the most beautiful cities in North America is built on a series of hills beside a wide bay of sparkling blue water. It has a fresh, springlike climate for much of the year, but is also famous for the white sea fogs, which roll in from the Pacific Ocean.

It was Spanish colonialists from Mexico who first built settlements here, seizing the land from Native Americans. In 1776 they built a military post, or *presidio,* on the bay and also a Roman Catholic mission called San Francisco de Asis. Another settlement called Yerba Buena was completed in 1836.

Grand Avenue in San Francisco was a bustling street. People came to spend their newly found fortunes if they had been successful in gold mining.

GOLDRUSH!

In 1846 California came under United States rule, and in May 1848 the little town of San Francisco had about 900 inhabitants. But by the end of the following year, this figure had risen to over 20,000!

Gold had been discovered in California. Miners rushed to San Francisco. Five hundred sailing ships lay at anchor in the bay. Newly won fortunes were lost in gambling dens and drunken miners were gunned down in the muddy streets in those lawless days.

THE SHAKING CITY

Over the years, the people of San Francisco settled

– SITTING ON A BOMB

down. But their city had another kind of problem - the land it was built on. There were severe earth tremors in 1839, 1865, and in 1868, when five people died.

The Californians realized that they had a problem here. They built their hillside houses from timber, using local redwood trees. It was known that timber buildings survived earthquakes better than brick ones. Geologists studied local rock formations and carried out regular surveys, carefully measuring movements of the crust along the San Andreas Fault.

COUNTDOWN TO DISASTER

By the year 1906, San Francisco had grown into the largest city west of the Missouri River, with a population of over 415,000. Its steep streets teemed with Chinese laborers, with European sailors, with wealthy American merchants and their wives.

Cable cars had first been tested in the city in 1873. Now the first cars honked their way through the crowds of office workers. Tall sailing vessels still entered the harbor through the narrow strait called the Golden Gate, carrying all kinds of cargoes from China, Japan, Australia, and Europe. The city thrived.

However, the Pacific Plate and the North American Plate were still jostling against each other, setting up strains along 267 miles (430 km) of the San Andreas Fault. Something had to give, as it had done so often in the rock systems of California. The difference this time was that hundreds of thousands of people were now living here, at one of the weakest points in the earth's crust.

APRIL 18, 1906

On this morning, the city was strangely quiet. Dogs, with their better sense of hearing than humans, were restless. Snakes left their burrows in the ground in daylight, apparently unafraid of being seen.

At 12 minutes and 6 seconds past 5:00 A.M., Pacific Standard Time, most people were still asleep in their beds. *But what happened next, and over the following days, is remembered as one of the worst natural disasters in world history.*

Horses and other animals react quickly to sounds and signs that humans may not even notice.

The population of San Francisco grew quickly once gold was discovered, and the city expanded.

WHAT HAPPENED NEXT?

WAS THE CITY COMPLETELY DESTROYED?

What happens in a major earthquake? A great shock occurs deep beneath the earth's surface, at a point called the focus. Shock waves travel outward from this point. The surface area directly above the focus is called the epicenter – and that is where the greatest damage occurs.

Buildings shake and tumble. Great cracks appear in the streets and gas and water pipes burst. And the tremors do not end quickly. For hours, days, months, and years dangerous aftershocks continue as the earth settles down.

had invented an earthquake recorder (a seismograph) and had set up a worldwide network for predicting earthquakes.

We know that by now the San Andreas Fault had been surveyed for 55 years. Did the seismologists see the telltale signs of an approaching disaster and warn that trouble lay ahead? Did the city council manage to evacuate people so that lives were saved? Did the fact that most housing was made of timber prevent serious accidents?

Did the earthquake miss the city? Were the buildings earthquake-proof?

WAS THE CITY FLOODED?

San Francisco is a port and owes it existence to the Pacific Ocean. And the Pacific is the home of some of the world's worst tsunamis. These can sweep along the seabed at over 460 miles (750 km) per hour and reach towering heights when they crash into a coastline.

Did a vast wave sweep across San Francisco Bay, sinking the ships in the harbor? Most of the city's buildings were on high ground, it is true. They would have been safe from flooding. But what about the waterfront and downtown streets? Were dockside buildings swept into the raging sea? Were dockworkers drowned as they reported for their morning shift? Were warehouses containing the city's food supplies destroyed?

Tidal waves are not uncommon in the Pacific. Did a huge wave engulf the city?

DID THE CITY ESCAPE DAMAGE?

Earthquakes have occurred throughout history. Around the world, about 100 major, and thousands of minor, earthquakes happen each year. The Chinese had invented a machine that showed where an earthquake was taking place as early as A.D. 132. By the year 1906, modern science was already making progress in investigating earthquakes. An English seismologist (or earthquake expert) named John Milne had already done valuable work studying tremors in Japan. He

On the morning of April 18, 1906, the people of San Francisco were rudely awakened. *Dogs were barking and trying to run away. Horses were panicking and kicking. And even the birds were startled and flying in circles.*

WHAT WAS HAPPENING IN SAN FRANCISCO?

WAS THERE A GREAT FIRE?

Did a gas explosion start off a great fire across the city? If water pipes burst as well the gas mains, it is often hard for firefighters to obtain enough water to put out fires. Could the horse-drawn fire engines of those days manage to get up the steep streets and cross cracked roadways at speed?

Did a terrible fire destroy the town's business district? Did it spread into the suburbs? Remember, most of the houses were built of wood. Did flames reach into the surrounding countryside, sparking off the century's worst forest fire?

If the gas mains were ruptured, fire could easily spread across the city and beyond.

The risk to life is immense. People may be buried alive in the debris or be hit by falling rubble. They may be killed in explosions or be forced to drive off the road. They may be made homeless or sick, or starve because supplies of food cannot get through. Is this what happened in San Francisco?

Earthquakes vary in intensity, and some cause more damage than others. Was this earthquake so severe that the entire city was destroyed?

WHAT REALLY HAPPENED TO SAN FRANCISCO?

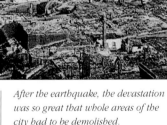

The earthquake destroyed buildings, leaving many people homeless.

San Francisco was hit by a severe earthquake. Its force was 8.3 on the Richter scale (the method by which we now measure shock waves at the surface). The main tremor lasted just one minute, five seconds, but was followed by many powerful aftershocks.

The terrible shaking turned the waterfront area into a trembling quicksand, into which the foundations of buildings collapsed.

THE GREAT BLAZE

At about nine in the morning, a woman in the city decided to make some breakfast and coffee, to steady her nerves. She lit a gas stove, which promptly exploded.

For three days, a terrible fire blazed. The army took over the city and dynamited whole streets to prevent the fire from spreading.

About 200,000 people fled to Golden Gate Park. Fifty thousand more camped in the grounds of the old *presidio*.

In all, at least 500 people were killed, including two thieves who were shot for looting.

After the earthquake, a team led by a geologist named Harry Fielding Reid studied the San Andreas Fault once more. It had

Opera singer Enrico Caruso sang to calm the terrified inhabitants of San Francisco as the earthquake raged.

After the earthquake, the devastation was so great that whole areas of the city had to be demolished.

shifted by about 20 feet (6 m). Some scientists claimed that this was the result of the earthquake, but most realized it was the cause.

LESSONS OF 1906

Great advances have been made since 1906. Buildings in modern San Francisco and Los Angeles are now specially designed to better withstand earthquakes. Stresses and strains in the rock can now be measured with laser beams. Movements in the earth's crust can even be surveyed from space.

But nothing can stop earthquakes happening. San Francisco was rocked again by the Loma Prieta disaster of 1989, and Los Angeles was shaken by a terrible earthquake in 1994. The powerful forces deep inside the Earth are better understood – but they cannot be tamed.

Modern buildings are specially designed to withstand earthquakes.

INDEX